# BEI GRIN MACHT SICH IHR
# WISSEN BEZAHLT

- Wir veröffentlichen Ihre Hausarbeit,
  Bachelor- und Masterarbeit

- Ihr eigenes eBook und Buch -
  weltweit in allen wichtigen Shops

- Verdienen Sie an jedem Verkauf

## Jetzt bei www.GRIN.com hochladen
## und kostenlos publizieren

Jutta Mahlke

# London Study Stops on Guy Fawkes

**Eine virtuelle Lern- und Übungswerkstatt (Hot Potatoes) mit besonderer Berücksichtigung des Present Perfect**

GRIN Verlag

**Bibliografische Information der Deutschen Nationalbibliothek:**

Die Deutsche Bibliothek verzeichnet diese Publikation in der Deutschen National-
bibliografie; detaillierte bibliografische Daten sind im Internet über http://dnb.d-
nb.de/ abrufbar.

**Impressum:**

Copyright © 2008 GRIN Verlag GmbH
Druck und Bindung: Books on Demand GmbH, Norderstedt Germany
ISBN: 978-3-640-22396-1

**Dieses Buch bei GRIN:**

http://www.grin.com/de/e-book/119250/london-study-stops-on-guy-fawkes

**GRIN - Your knowledge has value**

Der GRIN Verlag publiziert seit 1998 wissenschaftliche Arbeiten von Studenten, Hochschullehrern und anderen Akademikern als eBook und gedrucktes Buch. Die Verlagswebsite www.grin.com ist die ideale Plattform zur Veröffentlichung von Hausarbeiten, Abschlussarbeiten, wissenschaftlichen Aufsätzen, Dissertationen und Fachbüchern.

**Besuchen Sie uns im Internet:**

http://www.grin.com/

http://www.facebook.com/grincom

http://www.twitter.com/grin_com

## Gymnasien und Gesamtschulen NRW

Klasse 6, Gymnasium [G8]

Unterrichtsentwurf im Fach Englisch

## Thema der Unterrichtsreihe:
Around London (Unit 2)

## Thema der Unterrichtsstunde:
*Study Stops around London* on *Guy Fawkes* - Eine virtuelle Lernwerkstatt zur vielseitigen thematisch und strukturell vertieften Übung mit besonderer Berücksichtigung des *Present Perfect* (*Hot Potatoes* – Übungsstationen) und interkultureller Orientierung von London's historischen *Famous Sights*.

# 1. Geplanter Verlauf der Unterrichtsreihe

| Einheit (Std.) | Thema: Sequenz und Einheit |
|---|---|
| **Lead-In** | Gewinnen eines Überblicks über die Stadt London anhand der Erarbeitung des Stadtplans durch das kommunikative Sprachlernspiel „I spy from the London Eye" |
| **1. Sequenz (4 Std.)** | **London's Most Famous Sights** |
| 1. (2 Std.) | Sightseeing in London (Part 1) – Gruppenpuzzle und Internetrecherche |
| 2. (1 Std.) | Sightseeing in London (Part 2) - Teampräsentationen der Stationen „Hyde Park" und „The Tower of London" unter Berücksichtigung spezieller Peerfeedbackkriterien |
| 1 Std.) | Sightseeing in London (Part 3) -Teampräsentationen der Sights „Madame. Tussaud's" und „Buckingham Palace" als Poster |
| **2. Sequenz (4 Std.)** | **Visitors to London: Present Perfect und Past Participle** |
| 1. (1 Std.) | Grammar Detectives in der Textbuchgeschichte – Erwerbsorientierte Einführung der Form und Verwendung des Present Perfect in positiven und negativen Aussagesätzen unter besonderer Berücksichtigung des Past Partciple von regelmäßigen und unregelmäßigen Verben |
| 2. (1 Std.) | Have you ever? Fragen im Present Perfect |
| 3. (1 Std.) | Study Stops around London - Eine virtuelle Lernwerkstatt zur thematischen und strukturellen Übung unter besonderer Berücksichtigung des Present Perfect (Hot Potatoes - Übungsstationen) |
| | **2. Klassenarbeit** |

**Stundenvoraussetzung[1]:**

---

[1]Anm. der Aut.: Die SUS haben bereits Erfahrungen mit Internetrecherche zum Thema London gesammelt. Ihnen fehlte zu dem Zeitpunkt ihr bestellter Multimediatrainer zum Textbuch Camden Town 2, um insbesondere die Grammatik trainieren zu können. Hinzu kommt der landeskundliche Anlass des Tags. Die vereinbarte und kurzfristig vorbereitete Lernumgebung, auch für mich eine Premiere mit Hot Potatoes 6.2 im Klassenverband zu üben, kann zwar keinen vollwertigen Ersatz, soll aber lernerzentrierte Abhilfe und vielseitige Übungserfolge schaffen und sollte auch als ein derartiger (mutiger) Versuch weitgehend ohne Programmiervorkenntnisse gewertet werden. Ich habe rein konstruktivistischen Annahmen Folge geleistet, auf effektive Arbeit (in diesem Fall nur ca 15-20 Minuten, d.h. ca. 3-5 Übungen) auf der eingerichteten Plattform lässt sich hoffen, nur ein Beispiel mit jeweils maximal 3 Aufgaben (Download der empfehlenswerten Autoren Software für Lehrer: www.hotpotatoes.de). Diese Aufgaben stellen nur ein Beispiel dar, für diese Klasse eine Lernwerkstatt zu dieser Stunde, mehr nicht! Ein Versuch eben.

## 2. Ziele der Unterrichtsstunde

### 2.1 Übergeordnetes Lernziel

Die SuS sollen gemeinsam in einer virtuellen Lernumgebung (Lernwerkstatt – *study stops*) im eigenen Tempo die Fertigkeiten und Kenntnisse der Einheit „*Around London*" bis zur Geläufigkeit in neuen vertieften Zusammenhängen anwenden und weitgehend selbständig erweitern, üben und kontrollieren können.

### 2.2 Wesentliche Teillernziele

#### 2.2.1 Kognitive Lernziele

Die SuS sollen minimal zwei (maximal: alle) der folgenden Fertigkeiten erweitern:

➤ *Guy Fawkes* und die Traditionen des Tages in England kennenlernen. (interkulturelles Orientierungswissen)

➤ den Chant „*Please to remember the 5th of November*" in Elementen auswendig und ausdrucksvoll sprechen können.

➤ das *present perfect* in neuen Zusammenhängen verwenden können. (Grammatik)

➤ *past participles* der regelmäßigen und unregelmäßigen Verben kennen und verwenden können. (Grammatik)

➤ die Satzstellung von Fragen und Aussagen im *present perfect* in neuen Zusammenhängen verwenden können. (Struktur)

#### 2.2.2 Methodisches Lernziel

Die SuS sollen

➤ die vereinbarten gegebenen Aufgabenapparate am PC bearbeiten können.

#### 2.2.3 Sozial – affektives Lernziel

Die SuS sollen

➤ in eigenem Tempo selbstbestimmt üben

➤ den eigenen Lernfortschritt kontrollieren können.

# 3. Hausaufgaben

### 3.1 Hausaufgaben zur Stunde:
> Lest den Text „The Queen's House in the Tower of London and the Gunpower Plot",
unterstreicht das Present Perfect und lernt den Vers auswendig!

### 3.2 Hausaufgaben der Stunde:
(entfällt hier, freiwillige Übung an den study stops auch am heimischen PC offline möglich)

# 4. Geplanter Verlauf der Unterrichtsstunde

| Unterrichtsphase | Sach- und Verhaltensaspekte | Arbeits- und Sozialform | Medien |
|---|---|---|---|
| **Einstieg** | | frontal | |
| ►Warm Up | ➢ SuS sprechen den Chant rhythmisch vor und nach. (L. moderiert: soft, whisper, louder ... groups etc..) L. korrigiert present perfect marks | HV, chorisch | AB, analoge Datei, Beamer |
| ►Aufgreifen von Vorwissen aus der Vorstunde und erarbeitenden Hausaufgabe 5-10 min | ➢ L.: What do British Children traditionally do today? (according to the text) [e.g.: When they have collected enough pennies, ...] <br> ➢ SuS geben den Inhalt anhand von Impulsen wieder. [Tell us all about Guy Fawkes! What happened in the Queen's House on Nov. 5$^{th}$? Have you ever heard of Guy Fawkes? Do you agree with King James? Would you have hanged or helped Guy?] <br> ➢ SuS lösen die Drag&Drop Übung. | | Study Stop Drag&Drop Guy Fawkes |
| **Hinführung** <br> **5 min** <br> ► Demonstration | ➢ L. demonstriert die Arbeit mit den Study Stops an einigen Beispielen. <br> ➢ SuS bearbeiten die Beispiele am eigenen PC. | ge UG | Beamer PCs White-board (+ Marker) |
| **Erarbeitung** <br> **20 min** <br> ►durch differen-ziertes, program-miertes Üben <br> ►durch Feedback/ Selbstkontrolle | ➢ L. eröffnet die Erarbeitung im Netzwerk und beantwortet Fragen (moderiert). <br> ➢ SuS üben differenziert an den Study Stops. L. berät. <br> ➢ SuS überprüfen ihre Erarbeitungen anhand der Check und Feedback Funktionen. <br> ➢ *Bonus für sehr leistungsstarke SuS[2] | EA/PA 4 je dreifach gestufte Übungs-stationen mit Feedback zur Selbstkontrolle | Interaktive Hot-Potatoe websheets (Jmix, Cloze text, Drag&Drop , Masher) |
| **Sicherung** <br> **5-10 min** <br> ►durch Feedback (Austausch) | ➢ SuS stellen ihre Ergebnisse vor. <br> ➢ L-impulse und Feedback (Moderation) | presentations ent UG ge UG | SuS PC/ Beamer im Master Eye System |
| Stellen der Hausaufgabe | <u>Aufgabenstellung:</u> Relax! Don't work too hard! If you want to practice, feel free to download the free study stops. Write down the URL. | | URL |

# 5. Didaktisch – methodischer Kommentar

## 5.1 Sachstruktureller Entwicklungsstand der Lerngruppe

Den Rahmen der Reihe bildet das Textbuch Camden Town 2, dessen Teile A und B der Unit 2 bereits behandelt wurden. Daher sind Present Perfect und Past Participle in Form und Gebrauch in Aussage- und Fragesätzen bekannt. Die SuS sind mit den Textbuchfamilien und einigen Sehenswürdigkeiten Londons vertraut und an historischen Fakten, insbesondere im Rahmen der eigenen Präsentationen, interessiert. Guy Fawkes wurde bereits im „Tower of London" erwähnt.

## 5.2 Anbindung an den Lehrplan

Gemäß dem Kernlehrplan (G8) geben die SuS anhand des Anlasses Guy Fawkes Informationen aus adaptierten authentischen Texten wieder, die teilweise bereits bei der Internetrecherche zum „Tower of London" vorgetragen wurden. Der neue Übungstext bezieht sich auf bekannte und neue Inhalte zu Alltagleben von bekannten Schulkindern, Sightseeing und ansatzweise auch Shopping in London. Relevante neue Grammatik wird angewandt und gefestigt. Der rhythmische Chant „Please to remember the 5th of November" kann in Elementen auswendig vorgetragen werden. Alle Fertigkeiten werden geschult, interkulturelle und kommunikative Kompetenzen vertieft.

## 5.3 Didaktisch – methodische Überlegungen

Binnendifferenzierende Übungen zu Inhalt und Grammatik der bisher erarbeiteten Einheit bieten sich zur Vorbereitung auf die Arbeit an. Die Größe und Heterogenität der Klasse, sowie deren Vertrautheit im Umgang mit PC, Internet und Textverarbeitung (Medienkompetenz) lassen einen sinnvollen Einsatz der Übungen erwarten. Motivierend ist, dass der Multimediatrainer des Lehrwerks, den die SuS individuell zum Workbook bestellt hatten, noch nicht geliefert wurde, worauf ich die Erstellung von Hot Potatoes Worksheets (führende Autorensoftware für leistungsstarke webbasierte einfache und komplexe Übungen, die browserunabhängig auch Offline in vollem Umfang und geringer Größe funktionieren) anbot, wir diese vereinbarten, sodass sie das Leitmedium darstellen. Es wird dabei weitgehend vom konstruktiven Lerner ausgegangen, der auch bei programmierten Übungen den Lernprozess steuernd in die eigene Hand nimmt. Der Lehrer organisiert den Lernprozess, berät und moderiert, während die SuS im eigenen Tempo mit Lernhilfen von study stop zu study stop navigieren.

Die Übungen gliedern sich im wesentlichen in fünf Bereiche, Leseverstehen in Lückentext und Multiple Choice, Wortschatz und Grammatik (Partizip Perfekt Übungen), Strukturübungen zur Satzstellung im Present Perfect (Zuordnung und Drag & Drop) und multimediale landeskundliche Informationen zum historischen Text zum heutigen Anlass „Guy Fawkes". Sie sind in Umfang und Schwierigkeitsgrad in je drei Stufen gestaffelt. Das programmierte automatische Feedback der webworksheets, die hier „study stops" genannt werden, ermöglicht in einem jeweils vorgegebenen Zeitlimit maximale Übungserfolge und komplexe individuelle schnelle Rückmeldungen, ohne online arbeiten zu müssen. Theoretisch könnten die Ergebnisse ausgedruckt werden. Sinnvoller ist jedoch, dass die Übungen abgespeichert und auch zur späteren Wiederholung am eigenen PC heruntergeladen werden können.

## 6. Literaturliste

- Berkefeld, Astrid: *London's Most Famous Sights* – Ein Gruppenpuzzle für die Klassen 6 und 7, RAAbits Englisch, Einzelmaterial 144, Oktober 2007
- Camden Town (Gymnasium) Textbook 2, Diesterweg, Braunschweig, 2005
- Camden Town (Gymnasium) Lernideen & Materialien 2, Diesterweg, Braunschweig, 2005
- Camden Town (Gymnasium) Workbook 2, Diesterweg, Braunschweig, 2005
- Sabine Doff, Friederike Klippel: Englisch Didaktik, Praxishandbuch für die Sekundarstufe I und II, Cornelsen, 2008
- Haß, Frank (Hrsg.) Fachdidaktik Englisch, Ernst Klett Verlag GmbH, Stuttgart, 2006
- MSSWF: Sekundarstufe I. Gymnasium Englisch. Kernlehrplan (G8), 2007
- MSSWF: Richtlinien und Lehrpläne für das Gymnasium - Sekundarstufe I - in Nordrhein-Westfalen – Englisch, unver. Nachdruck, 2003
- Ziegésar, Detlef und Margaret: Einführung von Grammatik im Englischunterricht, Oldenbourg, München, 1992
- Guy Fawkes – A BIOGRAPHY; http://www.britannia.com/history/g-fawkes.html (27.10.2008)
- http://www.toweroflondon.com/kids

## 7. Anhang

- URL: http://homepage.ruhr-uni-bochum.de/Jutta.Mahlke/html/first.htm
- http://homepage.ruhr-uni-bochum.de/Jutta.Mahlke/html/around_london__year_2__-_jm_st.html
- Worksheet und Lösung zur Hausaufgabe zur Stunde

# The Queen 's House in the Tower of London and the Gunpowder Plot

- The Queen's House looks nothing like the other buildings inside the Tower. That's because it was made in a different style. While most of the buildings are stone, the Queen's House is made of wood. And where the other towers are tall, the Queen's House only has floors or stories. Isn't that a funny name when you think of it? Stories?

There was a huge fire long ago, which was called the Great Fire of London, and a lot of the houses in the city of London have caught fire because they were made of wood. The Queen's House was inside the stone walls of the Tower of London, therefore it was safe.

That makes it the only surviving house from that time!

But wait! They've told more interesting things about this house and history ... If you live in England you 've heard the very famous story of Guy Fawkes. For those of you who live elsewhere, Guy Fawkes was a man who tried to blow up the English Houses of Parliament. Imagine that!

He and some of his friends decided to dig a tunnel under Parliament. They rolled 36 barrels of gunpowder into the basement and planned to kill King James that way on November 5th, because he was Scottish. However, just before it was time to light the fuses to the gunpowder the King discovered the plot. Somebody sent the famous Monteagle letter, that told the Baron Monteagle, a member of parliament, about the plan on October 26th 1605.

Later Lord Chamberlain searched the parliament buildings with Monteagle. In the cellar they arrested Guy Fawkes and took him to the Tower of London as a prisoner. At the Tower - in fact in a hall known as the Council Chamber inside of the Queen's House – Guy confessed his plans to blow up Parliament and he told them seven more names. Guy Fawkes and three of his friends were tortured and hanged on January 31st, 1606.

Now, every November 5th Guy Fawkes Day is celebrated in England. Boys and girls get an old suit or maybe an old pair of dad's pants and an old jacket and stuff it with straw to make a straw figure that looks like Guy Fawkes. If they can get a hat they put that on, too. This figure is called a Guy. It's something like a scarecrow. The children then put the guy in a wooden cart and take him door to door asking people for "A penny for the Guy, please."

When they have collected enough pennies they go and buy fireworks ... rockets, and sparklers and bangers. As soon as it gets dark everyone, children and adults, build a huge bonfire with wood and sticks, and they throw the straw Guy on it and set the bonfire alight.

As the straw Guy burns up fireworks are set off and everyone chants a rhyme:

**Please to[3] remember the 5th of November**

**gunpowder, treason and plot.**

**We know of no reason**

**why gunpowder treason**

**should ever be forgot.**

. **Task:** Read the text, mark all present perfect sentences and try to memorize the rhyme!

---

[3] TIPP: Auch bekannt als: Remember, remember … (Illustration der Seite hilfreich, kann mit Lücken und Aufgaben versehen werden)

# The Queen 's House in the Tower of London and the Gunpowder Plot

- The Queen's House looks nothing like the other buildings inside the Tower.That's because it was made in a different style.While most of the buildings are stone, the Queen's House is made of wood. And where the other towers are tall, the Queen's House only has floors or stories. Isn't that a funny name when you think of it? Stories?

There was a huge fire long ago, which was called the Great Fire of London, and a lot of the houses in the city of London have caught fire because they were made of wood. The Queen's House was inside the stone walls of the Tower of London, therefore it was safe.

That makes it the only surviving house from that time!

But wait! They've told more interesting things about this house and history ... If you live in England you've heard the very famous story of Guy Fawkes. For those of you who live elsewhere, Guy Fawkes was a man who tried to blow up the English Houses of Parliament. Imagine that!

He and some of his friends decided to dig a tunnel under Parliament. They rolled 36 barrels of gunpowder into the basement and planned to kill King James that way on November 5$^{th}$, because he was Scottish. However, just before it was time to light the fuses to the gunpowder the King discovered the plot. Somebody sent the famous Monteagle letter, that told the Baron Monteagle, a member of parliament, about the plan on October 26$^{th}$ 1605.

Later Lord Chamberlain searched the parliament buildings with Monteagle. In the cellar they arrested Guy Fawkes and took him to the Tower of London as a prisoner. At the Tower - in fact in a hall known as the Council Chamber inside of the Queen's House – Guy confessed his plans to blow up Parliament and he told them seven more names. Guy Fawkes and three of his friends were tortured and hanged on January 31$^{st}$,1606.

Now, every November 5$^{th}$ Guy Fawkes Day is celebrated in England. Boys and girls get an old suit or maybe an old pair of dad's pants and an old jacket and stuff it with straw to make a straw figure that looks like Guy Fawkes. If they can get a hat they put that on, too. This figure is called a Guy. It's something like a scarecrow. The children then put the guy in a wooden cart and take him door to door asking people for "A penny for the Guy, please."

When they have collected enough pennies they go and buy fireworks ... rockets, and sparklers and bangers. As soon as it gets dark everyone, children and adults, build a huge bonfire with wood and sticks, and they throw the straw Guy on it and set the bonfire alight.

As the straw Guy burns up fireworks are set off and everyone chants a rhyme:

**Please to remember the 5th of November**

**gunpowder, treason and plot.**

**We know of no reason**

**why gunpowder treason**

**should ever be forgot.**

. **Task:** Read the text, mark all present perfect sentences and try to memorize the rhyme!